Contents

What is a colony?

Buzz! A bee zooms by.

It is taking food to its colony.

A colony is a group of bees

that live together.

Plus

Animal Groups

A Colony of Bees

by Lucia Raatma

raintree

a Capstone company — publishers for children

Raintree is an imprint of Capstone Global Library Limited, a company incorporated in England and Wales having its registered office at 264 Banbury Road, Oxford, OX2 7DY – Registered company number: 6695582

www.raintree.co.uk
myorders@raintree.co.uk

Edited by Abby Colich
Designed by Tracy McCabe
Original illustrations © Capstone Global Library Limited 2020
Picture research by Eric Gohl
Production by Kathy McColley
Originated by Capstone Global Library Ltd
Printed and bound in India

978 1 4747 8525 9 (hardback)
978 1 4747 8531 0 (paperback)

British Library Cataloguing in Publication Data
A full catalogue record for this book is available from the British Library.

Acknowledgements
We would like to thank the following for permission to reproduce photographs: Alamy: Scott Camazine, 15; Shutterstock: Azami Adiputera, 17, Banthoon Saeko, 11, bluedog studio, 19, Daniel Prudek, cover (isolated bee), Dredger, 13, Feri Istanto, back cover (bottom), 5, Ihor Bondarenko, 21, Pedro Turrini Neto, 7, rtbilder, cover, 1, StockMediaSeller, back cover (top), 9, StudioSmart, 2, background

Every effort has been made to contact copyright holders of material reproduced in this book. Any omissions will be rectified in subsequent printings if notice is given to the publisher.

All the internet addresses (URLs) given in this book were valid at the time of going to press. However, due to the dynamic nature of the internet, some addresses may have changed, or sites may have changed or ceased to exist since publication. While the author and publisher regret any inconvenience this may cause readers, no responsibility for any such changes can be accepted by either the author or the publisher. .

Bees build a nest for the colony to live in. The nests are in trees or in the ground. Some are under roofs or other covered areas.

Bee jobs

Each bee has a job. Most colonies have one queen. Her job is to lay eggs. Drones are males. They mate with the queen. The queen lays many eggs.

queen bee

Worker bees are female.
They do many jobs. Some search
for food. They gather pollen
and nectar from flowers.
They take it back to the nest.

Workers also feed and
take care of young bees.
They feed and clean the queen.
Some workers clean the nest.
Other bees guard the nest.

young

worker bee

13

Working together

Some bees dance to tell others where to find food. They dance in the shape of an 8. The longer they dance, the further away the food is.

Guard bees protect the entrance of the nest. They watch out for predators. Some bees sting predators. Other bees bite them.

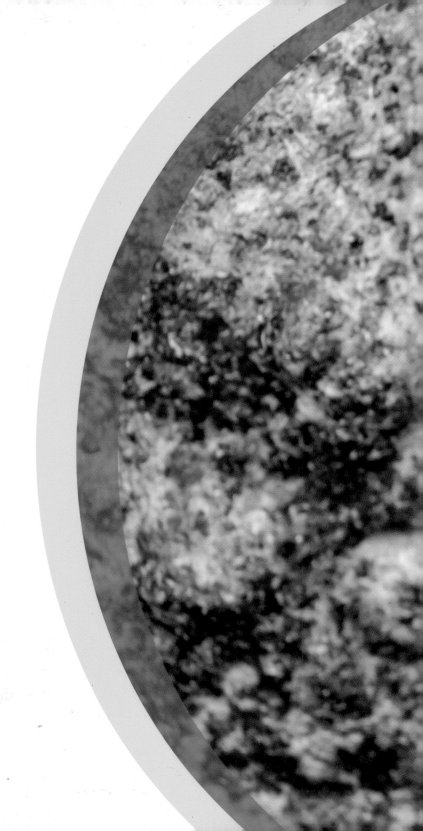

Some colonies get too crowded. The queen and some workers leave the nest. They build a new home. The old nest gets a new queen.

The need for bees

People need bees. Bees spread pollen from plant to plant. This helps plants to grow. People need those plants for food. They also use the honey that some bees make.

Glossary

mate join together to produce young

nectar sweet liquid found in many flowers

nest home where animals live and look after their young

pollen powder made by flowers to help them create new seeds

predator animal that hunts another animal for food

Find out more

Books

Bees and Wasps, James Maclaine (Usborne, 2013)

Bees and Wasps: Secrets of Their Busy Colonies (Amazing Animal Colonies), Sara L. Latta (Raintree, 2019)

Buzzing Bees (Smithsonian Little Explorer), Melissa Higgins (Raintree, 2020)

Websites

www.bbc.com/bitesize/articles/zx4ktv4
Learn more about why bees are attracted to flowers.

www.dkfindout.com/uk/animals-and-nature/insects/bee-colonies
Find out more about bee colonies.

Comprehension questions

1. What are some of the jobs of worker bees?
2. What happens when a nest gets too crowded?
3. Why do people need bees?

Index